This Book Belongs To:

Begun On:

Spell Done	Page

Spell Done	Page

Spell Done	Page

Spell Done	Page

Spell Done	Page

Spell Done	Page

What Are Spells

In a word, spells mean prayers. For some, it would look like magical prayers. Prayers, as everyone knows, affect the very fabric of reality itself when uttered and requested.

When there is a tear in this reality, a prayer repairs and restructures that part of the fabric once again, restoring it to its pristine, original self. This is one of the ways how the universe renews itself.

With each spell performed, every prayer, each word within every prayer (and even the very letters of the words of every prayer) has a precise meaning aimed for a precise effect. And, thus producing the final result of a successful spell casting.

Divine Intervention

When a spell is asked to be performed on your behalf, you are actually asking for a Divine intervention to take place in your situation. It is extremely important for you to understand that spells are not playthings to toy around.

The main point is that you know what the person is doing for you. In requesting a spell on your behalf, you must take the time to understand the type of spells the spell caster will perform.

Through the ages, there are many types of practices that can issue spells. Some of them would include Alchemy, Animism, Bonpo, Druidry, Egyptian Enochian, Hermeticism, Mantrik Hinduism, Hoodoo, Huna, Jewish Withcraft, Hermetic Qabalah, Nagualism, Quimbanda, Reiki, Santeria, Shamanism, Voodoo, Wicca, and many more listed around the world.

Protocols

In all of these styles, you have to understand that each requires a particular set of protocols and things you have to give up. The most important would be the rules that you will have to follow.

In some, the spells are accompanied by talismans and charms or amulets in order for these spells to work. This is not actually true for all of them, only on some intense, lower spells.

If these spells (or prayers, if you like) are performed correctly and all the protocols are in place, the request is granted and can have a dramatic impact on the intended person or situation. This happens even if the person is on the other side of the world.

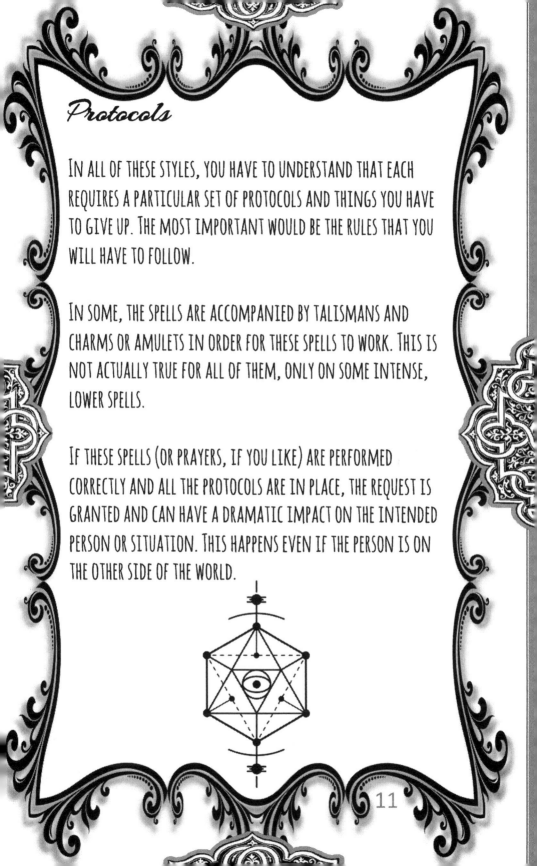

Angels and Entities

During the performance of spells, angels and other spirit entities are invoked to help make a success of these spells or prayers. Since these entities are pure energies themselves, spells are more in directing and guiding them to do things in aid of the spells.

There are other aids in casting spells. Witches use stones, herbs, candles, bones and others in order to attract the kind of energies needed for the present spell. These requests from free-floating entities and natural spirits have a price that witches must pay.

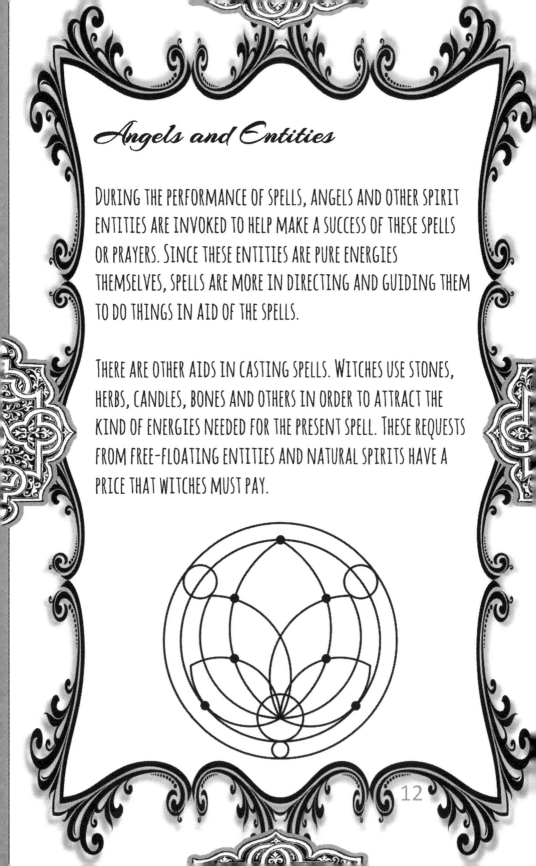

The payments are as varied as the spirits themselves. Some witches pay in actual blood drained from their bodies. Some require offerings. The spirits and entities feed off of these and become stronger. Consequently, your spell will then work.

Over time, the spell caster builds up rapport with certain entities and angels. Hence, their spells become more effective. When you ask for a spell from a witch, know that every effort is exerted for its success.

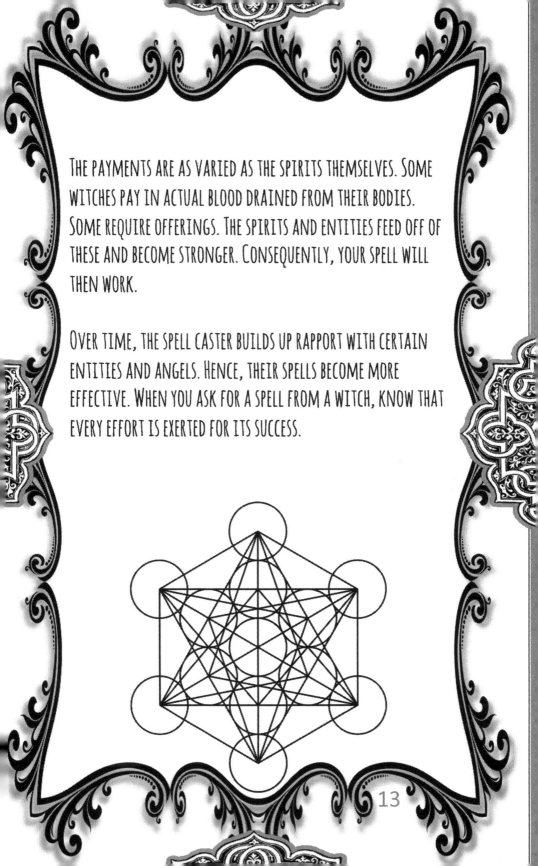

Spells & The Moon

Spells work best in tandem with natures' mysterious, magical and powerful objects. Of these, the moon is number one on the list for spell-givers.

The following are some refresher notes on spells and the phases of the moon.

New Moon / Dark Moon

Just like the full moon, the new moon (or dark moon) is the most opportune time to remove things from our lives. It is usually the time when you are most powerful in spell-giving.

This is a good time to reverse spells others have cast, ideal for banishing spells and focusing on the replacement of any negative effects all around.

However, keep in mind that when asking for something to be removed, there is a void left open. Ask for something positive and fill up that space.

To prevent a waxing influence on your spellwork, the banishing spells and rituals must be done before the beginning of the new moon. The most powerful time for spells is three days after the appearance of the new moon.

Black Moon

When two new moons appear during a single month, the second new moon is regarded as the stronger of the two. This is the best time to cast spells that deal on addiction.

Waxing Moon

The time of the waxing moon to full moon is the best time to cast spells on situations and events that concerns us.

The waxing moon is perfect for spellwork regarding success, protection, abundance, friendships, luck, new beginnings, and love.

The waxing moon is wonderful for good, constructive magic.

First Quarter

This is the mid-point between the new moon and the full moon. This is the time most ideal in focusing and meditating on attracting new positive things toward you. These things will grow as the moon waxes.

Waxing gibbous

This is the perfect time to focus on fruition and completion of your spellwork, and the time to focus and meditate on all the spellwork you did during the waxing phase.

This is also good to do any magical work on prophecy, protection or divination.

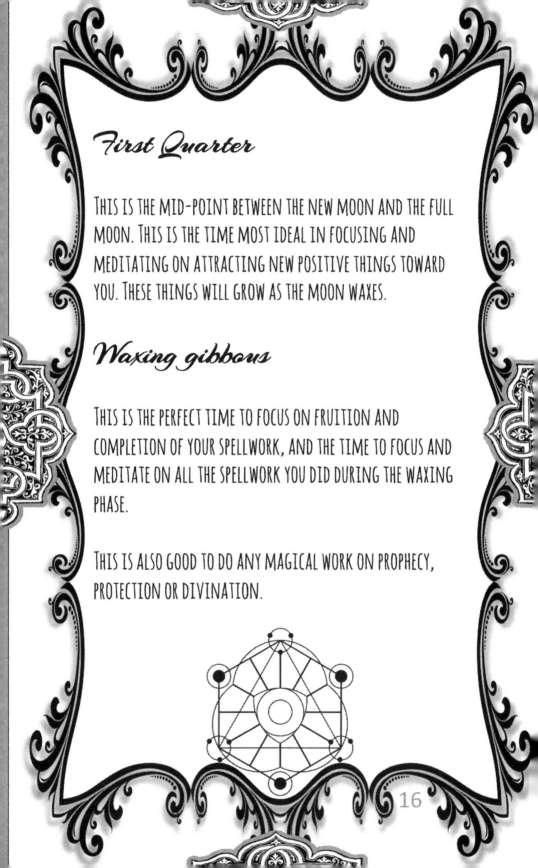

Full Moon

THIS IS THE TIME TO MEDITATE ON THE DIVINE POWER OF THE UNIVERSE AND PRAY THAT IT SHALL ALSO STRENGTHEN AND EMPOWER US. THE FULL MOON IMPARTS THE STRONGEST POWER FOR ALL INVOCATIONS AND SPELLS.

THIS IS THE TIME TO CAST YOUR MOST POWERFUL MAGIC SPELLS. TO AVOID A WANING INFLUENCE, CAST YOUR SPELLS AND DO YOUR RITUALS BEFORE THE EXACT TIME OF A FULL MOON.

Blue Moon

WHEN A MONTH HAS TWO FULL MOONS, THE 2ND FULL MOON IS DEEMED THE STRONGER AND MORE POWERFUL. FOR YOUR SPELLS AND RITUALS THAT NEED AN EXTRA KICK, THIS IS THE TIME TO DO THEM.

THIS IS ALSO THE TIME TO MEDITATE ON YOUR LIFE'S GOALS AND TO ASSESS YOUR SUCCESSES AND FAILURES.

Waning Gibbous

This is the best time to banish the things we don't want anymore in our lives. Plus, it is time to meditate on cleansing and removing all negativity around us.

Last Quarter

This is the time for ending things, much like the moon going to the end of its cycle. Focus and meditate on balancing your body's energies, replacing negatives with positives.

Waning Moon

The time of the waning to the new moon is also the best time to remove unwanted circumstances in our lives. Cast banishing spells against enemies, addictions, sickness, negativity, and evil. Cleanse yourself of the things you no longer need.

Love Spells for Varied Reasons

There is a wide range of reasons why a person casts spells on a fellow human being. Reasons may include love, money, success, or revenge to name a few. One reason branches out to varying methods depending on the nature of what the wisher wants to happen.

Take for example love . A method done in love spells varies according to what the wisher wants. Retrieve a love spell, gay love spell, unconditional love spell, and break-up or breaking spell are just a few examples of spells on The Subject of love.

For people who lost their loved ones, retrieve love spells help them get back their lovers. Unconditional love spells are used especially when one is doubtful of his lovers loyalty and wants to secure the presence of love in their relationship.

Meanwhile, gay love spells are effective in attracting someone of the same sex and break-up love spells for reviving your lovers' interest in you.

Let us give you an example of a simple love spell. This is best done on Friday and when the moon is in its fullest.

The things you will need are a sheet of lined paper, red pen or marker, letter envelope, your favorite perfume, your favorite shade of lipstick or a red one, and few pink or red flower petals.

- ➢ The first step is to write the good qualities you want your lover to have. Write these things on the sheet of paper using the red pen or marker.
- ➢ The next step is to spray the paper with your favorite perfume.
- ➢ This is followed by imagining a good scenario. Envision yourself happy and in-love while holding the flower petals in your right hand; keep thinking about this scene.
- ➢ The fourth step is to drop the petals into the envelope.
- ➢ Lastly, seal the envelope with paste and kiss it. Before kissing the envelope, make sure you have applied the red lipstick first.

With this spell, it is important to remember that this envelope should never be opened nor read by anyone else. Otherwise, the spell will be broken.

While many love spells require several items and are accompanied with ritual, the simple love spell is done simply by walking to a spot beneath your lover's bedroom window and then whispering his or her name three times to the night wind. This Simple love spell helps gain the love of someone; it is most effective during the night when it is a full moon.

It is important to note that the will of the wisher defines the power of the spell.

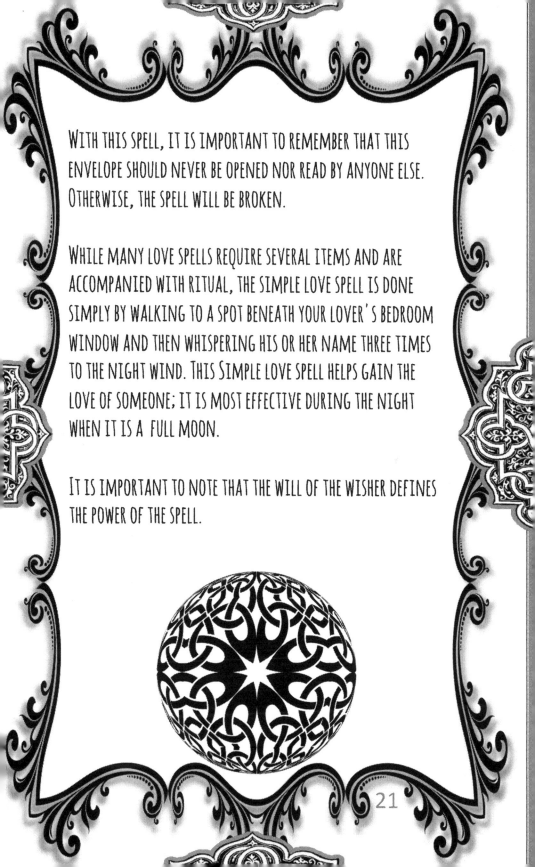

Preparing For A Spell

Casting spells is not just about reading incantations and using candles and incense. There is more to it than reading lines and waiting for the outcome.

For some, especially Wiccans, using or casting spells is a part of their religious belief. This could be an equivalent of a prayer. Casting spells is considered to be an intentional use of the universes' power that already exists around us.

Casting or using spells would require meditation and directing the spell-casters spiritual energy into the desired outcome. Directing your personal energy means that a person should have an understanding of the power within the person. For example, casting a spell may require some items like candles, etc.

The spell-caster should evoke imagery and visualize the goal while holding the items. This practice would direct the energy towards the items which would help in achieving the goals.

There are strict guidelines that should be followed when casting or using spells. Wiccans would follow the the Wiccan Rede which states that

Do What Ye Will, Harm Ye None.

This clearly states that Wiccans could perform rituals and spells but its effect or consequences should be recognized first. For harm done to others and nature, will return three-fold. Spell-casting cannot be used for anger, revenge, and jealousy.

Aside from being clear with your intensions, you should also be clear in what situation you will be using the spell. There are different kinds of spells, all depending on the situation. There are healing, love, energy, wealth, peace and other kinds of spells.

There are spells which can be modified to suit the needs and situation of the spell-caster. There are some spells which would require the spell-caster to use the exact words, while some would say that those spells which are spoken by the spell-caster's own words are more pure and powerful.

Spell-casting would also use different tools or methods. These tools would contain the energy which can be used to represent your desires and goals. There are different kinds of tools like oils, candles, cards, stones, runes, etc. Most of the times, the object used is something associated with the objective or intent. For example, if it is a money spell, loose change can be used as a tool.

The location where to cast the spell is also important. Wiccans believe that we are one with nature. They may have some rituals and practices which would require them to be with nature,

however, spell-casting can also be done privately. Some Wicca followers would often conduct their practices secretly, not only to avoid public persecution but to contain their energies and direct them towards their goal.

When casting a spell, it is important to keep in mind that we are using our energy and directing it to achieve a desired outcome. The universe is full of energy. Therefore, there could be negative energy which could interfere with how we use ours. Performing privately would ensure that our energy and our spell are not disturbed.

Another common problem among spell-casters is the timing. Some spells would require specific time to perform them. Adapting to time phase could be hard. There are some expert spell-catchers who would say that performing spells under a full moon, for instance, is not that important. It can increase the potency of the spell, but it is the intention which is more important. Directing our mind and spiritual energy towards our objective would be the determining factor on how effective our spells would be.

There are just so many Spells it is impossible to put them into a book for you. This is NOT our site but it has a great list of Beginner Spells so go to:

HTTP://BIT.LY/FreeWiccaSpells

DATE: CASTER:

NAME OF RITUAL OR SPELL :

PURPOSE :

PARTICIPANTS: DEITIES INVOKED:

WAXING			FULL MOON			WANING

DESCRIPTION

INGREDIENTS & EQUIPMENT

IMMEDIATE FEELINGS AND EFFECTS

IMPORTANT NOTES:

MANIFESTATION DATE:

RESULTS	EVENTS

DATE: CASTER:

NAME OF RITUAL OR SPELL :

PURPOSE :

PARTICIPANTS: DEITIES INVOKED:

WAXING			FULL MOON			WANING

DESCRIPTION

INGREDIENTS & EQUIPMENT

IMMEDIATE FEELINGS AND EFFECTS

IMPORTANT NOTES:

MANIFESTATION DATE:

RESULTS	EVENTS

Date: Caster:

Name of Ritual or Spell :

Purpose :

Participants: Deities Invoked:

WAXING	FULL MOON	WANING

DESCRIPTION

INGREDIENTS & EQUIPMENT

IMMEDIATE FEELINGS AND EFFECTS

IMPORTANT NOTES:

MANIFESTATION DATE:

RESULTS	EVENTS

DATE: CASTER:

NAME OF RITUAL OR SPELL :

PURPOSE :

PARTICIPANTS: DEITIES INVOKED:

WAXING	FULL MOON	WANING

DESCRIPTION

INGREDIENTS & EQUIPMENT

IMMEDIATE FEELINGS AND EFFECTS

IMPORTANT NOTES:

Results	Events

DATE: CASTER:
NAME OF RITUAL OR SPELL :

PURPOSE :

PARTICIPANTS: DEITIES INVOKED:

| WAXING | | FULL MOON | | | WANING | |

DESCRIPTION

INGREDIENTS &
EQUIPMENT

IMMEDIATE FEELINGS AND EFFECTS

IMPORTANT NOTES:

Manifestation Date:

Results	Events

Date: Caster:

Name of Ritual or Spell :

Purpose :

Participants: Deities Invoked:

| WAXING | | | FULL MOON | | | WANING |

DESCRIPTION

INGREDIENTS & EQUIPMENT

IMMEDIATE FEELINGS AND EFFECTS

IMPORTANT NOTES:

MANIFESTATION DATE:

RESULTS	EVENTS

DATE: CASTER:

NAME OF RITUAL OR SPELL :

PURPOSE :

PARTICIPANTS: DEITIES INVOKED:

WAXING	FULL MOON	WANING

DESCRIPTION

INGREDIENTS &
EQUIPMENT

IMMEDIATE FEELINGS AND EFFECTS

IMPORTANT NOTES:

MANIFESTATION DATE:

RESULTS	EVENTS

DATE: CASTER:
NAME OF RITUAL OR SPELL :

PURPOSE :

PARTICIPANTS: DEITIES INVOKED:

WAXING	FULL MOON	WANING

DESCRIPTION

INGREDIENTS & EQUIPMENT

IMMEDIATE FEELINGS AND EFFECTS

IMPORTANT NOTES:

MANIFESTATION DATE:

RESULTS	EVENTS

Date: Caster:

Name of Ritual or Spell :

Purpose :

Participants: Deities Invoked:

WAXING			FULL MOON			WANING

DESCRIPTION

INGREDIENTS &
EQUIPMENT

IMMEDIATE FEELINGS AND EFFECTS

IMPORTANT NOTES:

MANIFESTATION DATE:

RESULTS	EVENTS

DATE: CASTER:

NAME OF RITUAL OR SPELL :

PURPOSE :

PARTICIPANTS: DEITIES INVOKED:

WAXING	FULL MOON	WANING

DESCRIPTION

INGREDIENTS & EQUIPMENT

IMMEDIATE FEELINGS AND EFFECTS

IMPORTANT NOTES:

Manifestation Date:

Results	Events

DATE: CASTER:

NAME OF RITUAL OR SPELL :

PURPOSE :

PARTICIPANTS: DEITIES INVOKED:

WAXING			FULL MOON			WANING

DESCRIPTION

INGREDIENTS &
EQUIPMENT

IMMEDIATE FEELINGS AND EFFECTS

IMPORTANT NOTES:

MANIFESTATION DATE:

RESULTS	EVENTS

DATE: CASTER:

NAME OF RITUAL OR SPELL :

PURPOSE :

PARTICIPANTS: DEITIES INVOKED:

WAXING			FULL MOON		WANING	

DESCRIPTION

INGREDIENTS & EQUIPMENT

IMMEDIATE FEELINGS AND EFFECTS

IMPORTANT NOTES:

MANIFESTATION DATE:

RESULTS	EVENTS

Date: Caster:

Name of Ritual or Spell :

Purpose :

Participants: Deities Invoked:

WAXING			FULL MOON			WANING

DESCRIPTION

INGREDIENTS &
EQUIPMENT

IMMEDIATE FEELINGS AND EFFECTS

IMPORTANT NOTES:

MANIFESTATION DATE:

RESULTS	EVENTS

DATE: CASTER:

NAME OF RITUAL OR SPELL :

PURPOSE :

PARTICIPANTS: DEITIES INVOKED:

WAXING	FULL MOON	WANING

DESCRIPTION

INGREDIENTS & EQUIPMENT

IMMEDIATE FEELINGS AND EFFECTS

IMPORTANT NOTES:

MANIFESTATION DATE:

RESULTS	EVENTS

Date: Caster:

Name of Ritual or Spell :

Purpose :

Participants: Deities Invoked:

WAXING	FULL MOON	WANING

DESCRIPTION

INGREDIENTS &
EQUIPMENT

IMMEDIATE FEELINGS AND EFFECTS

IMPORTANT NOTES:

MANIFESTATION DATE:

RESULTS	EVENTS

DATE: CASTER:

NAME OF RITUAL OR SPELL :

PURPOSE :

PARTICIPANTS: DEITIES INVOKED:

| WAXING | | | FULL MOON | | | WANING |

DESCRIPTION

INGREDIENTS &
EQUIPMENT

IMMEDIATE FEELINGS AND EFFECTS

IMPORTANT NOTES:

MANIFESTATION DATE:

RESULTS	EVENTS

DATE: CASTER:

NAME OF RITUAL OR SPELL :

PURPOSE :

PARTICIPANTS: DEITIES INVOKED:

WAXING	FULL MOON	WANING

DESCRIPTION

INGREDIENTS & EQUIPMENT

IMMEDIATE FEELINGS AND EFFECTS

IMPORTANT NOTES:

MANIFESTATION DATE:

RESULTS	EVENTS

DATE: CASTER:
NAME OF RITUAL OR SPELL :

PURPOSE :

PARTICIPANTS: DEITIES INVOKED:

WAXING			FULL MOON			WANING

DESCRIPTION

INGREDIENTS &
EQUIPMENT

IMMEDIATE FEELINGS AND EFFECTS

IMPORTANT NOTES:

Results	Events

DATE: CASTER:

NAME OF RITUAL OR SPELL :

PURPOSE :

PARTICIPANTS: DEITIES INVOKED:

WAXING	FULL MOON	WANING

DESCRIPTION

INGREDIENTS & EQUIPMENT

IMMEDIATE FEELINGS AND EFFECTS

IMPORTANT NOTES:

MANIFESTATION DATE:

RESULTS	EVENTS

DATE: CASTER:

NAME OF RITUAL OR SPELL :

PURPOSE :

PARTICIPANTS: DEITIES INVOKED:

WAXING	FULL MOON	WANING

DESCRIPTION

INGREDIENTS & EQUIPMENT

IMMEDIATE FEELINGS AND EFFECTS

IMPORTANT NOTES:

MANIFESTATION DATE:

RESULTS	EVENTS

DATE: CASTER:

NAME OF RITUAL OR SPELL :

PURPOSE :

PARTICIPANTS: DEITIES INVOKED:

WAXING	FULL MOON	WANING

DESCRIPTION

INGREDIENTS &
EQUIPMENT

IMMEDIATE FEELINGS AND EFFECTS

IMPORTANT NOTES:

MANIFESTATION DATE:

RESULTS	EVENTS

DATE: CASTER:

NAME OF RITUAL OR SPELL :

PURPOSE :

PARTICIPANTS: DEITIES INVOKED:

WAXING	FULL MOON	WANING

DESCRIPTION

INGREDIENTS & EQUIPMENT

IMMEDIATE FEELINGS AND EFFECTS

IMPORTANT NOTES:

Manifestation Date:

Results	Events

DATE: CASTER:

NAME OF RITUAL OR SPELL :

PURPOSE :

PARTICIPANTS: DEITIES INVOKED:

WAXING	FULL MOON	WANING

DESCRIPTION

INGREDIENTS & EQUIPMENT

IMMEDIATE FEELINGS AND EFFECTS

IMPORTANT NOTES:

Manifestation Date:

Results	Events

DATE: CASTER:

NAME OF RITUAL OR SPELL :

PURPOSE :

PARTICIPANTS: DEITIES INVOKED:

WAXING	FULL MOON	WANING

DESCRIPTION

INGREDIENTS & EQUIPMENT

IMMEDIATE FEELINGS AND EFFECTS

IMPORTANT NOTES:

Manifestation Date:

Results	Events

DATE: CASTER:

NAME OF RITUAL OR SPELL :

PURPOSE :

PARTICIPANTS: DEITIES INVOKED:

WAXING			FULL MOON			WANING

DESCRIPTION

INGREDIENTS & EQUIPMENT

IMMEDIATE FEELINGS AND EFFECTS

IMPORTANT NOTES:

MANIFESTATION DATE:

RESULTS	EVENTS

DATE: CASTER:

NAME OF RITUAL OR SPELL :

PURPOSE :

PARTICIPANTS: DEITIES INVOKED:

WAXING			FULL MOON			WANING

DESCRIPTION

INGREDIENTS & EQUIPMENT

IMMEDIATE FEELINGS AND EFFECTS

IMPORTANT NOTES:

MANIFESTATION DATE:

RESULTS	EVENTS

DATE: CASTER:

NAME OF RITUAL OR SPELL :

PURPOSE :

PARTICIPANTS: DEITIES INVOKED:

WAXING	FULL MOON	WANING

DESCRIPTION

INGREDIENTS & EQUIPMENT

IMMEDIATE FEELINGS AND EFFECTS

IMPORTANT NOTES:

Manifestation Date:

Results	Events

DATE: CASTER:

NAME OF RITUAL OR SPELL :

PURPOSE :

PARTICIPANTS: DEITIES INVOKED:

WAXING			FULL MOON			WANING

DESCRIPTION

INGREDIENTS &
EQUIPMENT

IMMEDIATE FEELINGS AND EFFECTS

IMPORTANT NOTES:

MANIFESTATION DATE:

RESULTS	EVENTS

Date: Caster:

Name of Ritual or Spell :

Purpose :

Participants: Deities Invoked:

Waxing	Full Moon	Waning

DESCRIPTION

INGREDIENTS &
EQUIPMENT

IMMEDIATE FEELINGS AND EFFECTS

IMPORTANT NOTES:

MANIFESTATION DATE:

RESULTS	EVENTS

DATE: CASTER:

NAME OF RITUAL OR SPELL :

PURPOSE :

PARTICIPANTS: DEITIES INVOKED:

WAXING	FULL MOON	WANING

DESCRIPTION

INGREDIENTS & EQUIPMENT

IMMEDIATE FEELINGS AND EFFECTS

IMPORTANT NOTES:

MANIFESTATION DATE:

RESULTS	EVENTS

DATE: CASTER:

NAME OF RITUAL OR SPELL :

PURPOSE :

PARTICIPANTS: DEITIES INVOKED:

WAXING	FULL MOON	WANING

DESCRIPTION

INGREDIENTS & EQUIPMENT

IMMEDIATE FEELINGS AND EFFECTS

IMPORTANT NOTES:

Manifestation Date:

Results	Events

DATE: CASTER:

NAME OF RITUAL OR SPELL :

PURPOSE :

PARTICIPANTS: DEITIES INVOKED:

WAXING	FULL MOON	WANING

DESCRIPTION

INGREDIENTS &
EQUIPMENT

IMMEDIATE FEELINGS AND EFFECTS

IMPORTANT NOTES:

MANIFESTATION DATE:

RESULTS	EVENTS

DATE: CASTER:

NAME OF RITUAL OR SPELL :

PURPOSE :

PARTICIPANTS: DEITIES INVOKED:

WAXING	FULL MOON	WANING

DESCRIPTION

INGREDIENTS & EQUIPMENT

IMMEDIATE FEELINGS AND EFFECTS

IMPORTANT NOTES:

Manifestation Date:

Results	Events

DATE: CASTER:

NAME OF RITUAL OR SPELL :

PURPOSE :

PARTICIPANTS: DEITIES INVOKED:

WAXING	FULL MOON	WANING

DESCRIPTION

INGREDIENTS & EQUIPMENT

IMMEDIATE FEELINGS AND EFFECTS

IMPORTANT NOTES:

MANIFESTATION DATE:

RESULTS	EVENTS

DATE: CASTER:

NAME OF RITUAL OR SPELL :

PURPOSE :

PARTICIPANTS: DEITIES INVOKED:

WAXING	FULL MOON	WANING

DESCRIPTION

INGREDIENTS & EQUIPMENT

IMMEDIATE FEELINGS AND EFFECTS

IMPORTANT NOTES:

MANIFESTATION DATE:

RESULTS	EVENTS

DATE: CASTER:

NAME OF RITUAL OR SPELL :

PURPOSE :

PARTICIPANTS: DEITIES INVOKED:

WAXING			FULL MOON			WANING

DESCRIPTION

INGREDIENTS & EQUIPMENT

IMMEDIATE FEELINGS AND EFFECTS

IMPORTANT NOTES:

Manifestation Date:

Results	Events

DATE: CASTER:

NAME OF RITUAL OR SPELL :

PURPOSE :

PARTICIPANTS: DEITIES INVOKED:

WAXING	FULL MOON	WANING

DESCRIPTION

INGREDIENTS & EQUIPMENT

IMMEDIATE FEELINGS AND EFFECTS

IMPORTANT NOTES:

Manifestation Date:

Results	Events

DATE: CASTER:

NAME OF RITUAL OR SPELL :

PURPOSE :

PARTICIPANTS: DEITIES INVOKED:

WAXING	FULL MOON	WANING

DESCRIPTION

INGREDIENTS & EQUIPMENT

IMMEDIATE FEELINGS AND EFFECTS

IMPORTANT NOTES:

MANIFESTATION DATE:

RESULTS	EVENTS

DATE: CASTER:

NAME OF RITUAL OR SPELL :

PURPOSE :

PARTICIPANTS: DEITIES INVOKED:

WAXING		FULL MOON		WANING	

DESCRIPTION

INGREDIENTS & EQUIPMENT

IMMEDIATE FEELINGS AND EFFECTS

IMPORTANT NOTES:

Manifestation Date:

Results	Events

DATE: CASTER:

NAME OF RITUAL OR SPELL :

PURPOSE :

PARTICIPANTS: DEITIES INVOKED:

WAXING			FULL MOON			WANING

DESCRIPTION

INGREDIENTS &
EQUIPMENT

IMMEDIATE FEELINGS AND EFFECTS

IMPORTANT NOTES:

MANIFESTATION DATE:

RESULTS	EVENTS

DATE: CASTER:

NAME OF RITUAL OR SPELL :

PURPOSE :

PARTICIPANTS: DEITIES INVOKED:

WAXING			FULL MOON			WANING

DESCRIPTION

INGREDIENTS &
EQUIPMENT

IMMEDIATE FEELINGS AND EFFECTS

IMPORTANT NOTES:

MANIFESTATION DATE:

RESULTS	EVENTS

DATE: CASTER:

NAME OF RITUAL OR SPELL :

PURPOSE :

PARTICIPANTS: DEITIES INVOKED:

WAXING	FULL MOON	WANING

DESCRIPTION

INGREDIENTS & EQUIPMENT

IMMEDIATE FEELINGS AND EFFECTS

IMPORTANT NOTES:

MANIFESTATION DATE:

RESULTS	EVENTS

Time to grab a new book.
If You enjoyed this book, we hope
you will leave Us a great review.
Spiritual Awakening Portal Books

Made in the USA
San Bernardino, CA
27 February 2020